W9-BKO-700

GREENUP COUNTY PUBLIC LIBRARY
614 MAIN STREET
GREENUP, KY 41144

Oddhopper Opera

A BUG'S GARDEN OF VERSES

Kurt Cyrus

Voyager Books
Harcourt, Inc.

Orlando   Austin   New York   San Diego   Toronto   London

Copyright © 2001 by Kurt Cyrus

All rights reserved. No part of this publication may be reproduced or transmitted in any
form or by any means, electronic or mechanical, including photocopy, recording, or any
information storage and retrieval system, without permission in writing from the publisher.
Requests for permission to make copies of any part of the work should be submitted online
at www.harcourt.com/contact or mailed to the following address: Permissions Department,
Harcourt, Inc., 6277 Sea Harbor Drive, Orlando, Florida 32887-6777.

www.HarcourtBooks.com

First Voyager Books edition 2007
Voyager Books is a trademark of Harcourt, Inc., registered in
the United States of America and/or other jurisdictions.

The Library of Congress has cataloged the hardcover edition as follows:
Cyrus, Kurt.
Oddhopper opera: a bug's garden of verses/Kurt Cyrus.
p. cm.
Summary: A collection of poems about the activities of a variety
of different bugs which flourish in a garden from early spring to late fall.
1. Insects—Juvenile poetry. 2. Gardens—Juvenile poetry.
3. American poetry. [1. Insects—Poetry. 2. Gardens—Poetry.
3. Children's poetry, American.] I. Title.
PS 3553.Y49 B83 2001
811'.5421—dc21 99-6799
ISBN 978-0-15-202205-1
ISBN 978-0-15-205855-5 pb

A C E G H F D B

The display type was hand-lettered by Jane Dill.
The text type was set in Minister Light.
Manufactured by South China Printing Company, Ltd., China
Production supervision by Pascha Gerlinger
Designed by Lori McThomas Buley

Once upon a garden rotten,
Twice forlorn and half forgotten…

Drip—drip—cold and wet.
Winter isn't over yet.

Drip—drip—soaking, sopping,
Always dripping, never stopping.

Drip—drip—sound of thunder
Wakes a weevil way down under.

Drip—drip—burrow deep.
Wait for spring. Go back to sleep.

Popping hot peppers—it's sixty degrees!
Calling all oddhoppers! Aphids and bees,
Crickets and dung beetles, earwigs and fleas!
Great galloping grubs, get a whiff of that breeze!

We're hopping and kicking and thrashing and thumping,

Rooting and scooting and jabbing and jumping,

Bouncing and biting and buzzing and bumping,

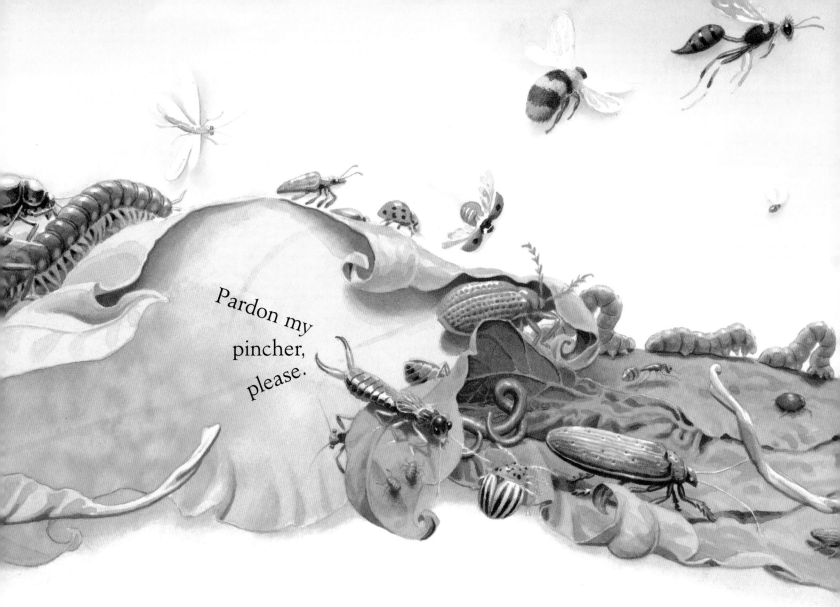

Pardon my pincher, please.

Bummer Beetle, on his back.
Bummer Beetle, dressed in black.
Bummer Beetle kicks and kicks—
Kicks his legs up, two, four, six.
Bummer Beetle cries and cries,
Waving, waving at the skies;
Praying, praying passing feet'll
Pity, pity Bummer Beetle.

Leafhopper sits
On a bump on a leaf—
That's not a bump!
It's a bug! Good grief!

Look at the leaf—
Is it blinking its eyes?
Eek! It's a katydid!
What a surprise!

Katydid, Katydid,
Better be quick—
You're standing on top
Of a walkingstick.

You, Mr. Stick,
Ought to pick a new spot!

You think that's a cucumber vine—

but it's not.

Bugs are digging—scoop it out.
Move it, boys, let's hack it out!
Front feet, back feet, scrape it out.
   Dig we must.
   Excuse our dust.
Black muck, brown muck, mix it up.
Watch it, boys, it's breaking up!
Punch it! Pat it! Patch it up!
   Bless my soul—
   It's time to roll.
Dung balls rolling—move 'em out!

Mama Pitter-Patter-Pede had half a hundred legs;
Just for fun, she took a run, and laid a hundred eggs.

Seven in the celer

Three upon a pepper plant,

through;

was tunneled clear

Twenty in a turnip that

a dozen in the dew,

thirty in the peas,

ten upon a butter bean, blowing in the breeze;

Nine that wobbled to the north,

eight that wobbled south ...

and one that wibble-wobbled into Bummer Beetle's mouth.

All of the snails are starting a race.
Give 'em some room! Give 'em some space!
Give 'em the go-ahead! Give 'em a cheer!
These are the things that they hanker to hear.
Give them a holler, a nod, and a nudge....
Give them a minute, and see if they budge.

Used to be a pollywog, and then I must have blinked—
Now I don't know *what* I am. My tail has gone extinct.
Legs are sticking out all over. Got a humpy back.
Not a lot to grin about—*GRAAAAAAAAK!*

Jeepers-creepers, where'd I get these big ol' bulgy eyes?
Can't believe the stuff I'm eating—maggots, worms, and flies.
Feeling kind of bloated. Guess I'll have another snack.
Slurp a little puddle scum—*GRAAAAAAAAAK!*

BOINK!

"Mama, hey Mama Bug, look overhead!
Why is the sky full of silvery thread?"
"It's there for whoever—for me and for you;
It's there for us *all*, Bugaboo."

"Mama, hey Mama! Oh, isn't it grand?
A silvery web waving over the land!"
"It waves at the butterflies up in the blue,
And also at *you*, Bugaboo."

"Mama, that fellow all covered with fuzz—
Why is he winking, the way that he does?"
  "For houseflies, and horseflies, and hover flies, too—
And *you*, Bugaboo. And for you."

"Mama, he's rubbing his big fuzzy gut.
Fuzzy looks hungry, but hungry for what?"
  "For anyone. Everyone. Who knows who?
For you, Bugaboo. For you."

BOINK!

I tried to take my skin off.
(How else am I to grow?)
I tried to take my skin off, but it
    wouldn't—let—go!

It held me and it hugged me,
That creepy, crawly skin.
It wrapped itself around me, and it
    kept—me—in!

We grappled in the artichokes
    and tumbled through the lettuce.
We wrestled in the spinach, where
    a spider tried to get us.

It crinkled! And it crackled! And
I kicked myself free!
So now it just…
    hangs there…
        staring at…
            me.

BOINK! "SOMEONE SAID SOMEONE FOUND SOMETHING DEAD!"

BOINK! "OFF WE GO! IS IT FAR, DO YOU KNOW?"

Through the tangle, softly gliding,
Comes a long, long tummy, sliding—
Just a belly, nothing more,
Except the eyes that come before,
And a mouth so wide and hollow,
No one knows what it might swallow.
Crickets? Weevils? Worms or slugs?
Juicy, slurpy spittlebugs?
Bouncing frogs, all slick and fat?
Garden fresh. You can't beat that!
How about some fuzzy mice?
Crunchy snails are always nice....
Sliding softly, here and gone,
A belly with a head stuck on.

Under the thunderheads, over the trails,
Rumbling, rumbling—here come the snails!
Slapping their slime at a furious pace—
Mrs. Molasses is leading the race.
Mr. Mistake is beginning to stray—
He's slipping! He's sliding! Get out of the way!

BOINK! "HERE WE ARE—WHERE'S THE FOOD? IS IT FAR?"   BOINK! "OH, MY HEAD! CAN'T WE SHAKE HANDS INSTEAD?"   BOINK!

Big tomato—juicy, fat.
Gonna make a major splat.

Stinkbug, smelly fellow, hiding in the ground.
Under cover, barely breathing, doesn't make a sound.
No one hears him. No one sees him. Only trouble is...
IT'S NEVER ANY SECRET WHERE A STINKBUG IS!

EAST THE EVIL PERFUME BLOWS...

BOINK! "GO! GO! GO! THERE'S A STINKBUG BELOW!"

BOINK! "ARE WE DONE? THIS IS NO LONGER FUN." BOINK! "UP AHEAD—SOMETHING BIG! SOMETHING DEAD!"

"Hey," says the fly, "you're an odd little guy.
They say you're my son, but I know it's a lie.
Where are your wings? And your legs, and things?
All that you're made of is fat little rings.
It's easy to see, and I'm sure you'll agree,
You can't be my kid. You look *nothing* like me."
"Oh, give me a break," says the son. "Goodness sake!
You once were a maggot yourself, you old fake!"

JUST ONE WHIFF, AND AWAY HE GOES.

STRAIGHT TO BUMMER BEETLE'S NOSE…

"I'm waiting, waiting, waiting,

and I haven't caught a thing,

Except a piece of purple from a butterfly's wing,

And dandelion seeds, about a dozen altogether,

Some fuzzy stuff—just worthless fluff—

a birdy's belly feather...."

"Well, look who's back! Just watch it, Jack. I'm spoiling for a fight!
You want your feather? Tell you what—I'll trade it for one bite!
I'm mad! I'm bad! I'm hungry, and you're not too big to catch.
Hey, watch that beak! Oh, Mama! *Eeek*—"

One spider down the hatch.

"Papa, O Papa Bug, where have you been?"
"A place I will never go back to again!"
"Papa, O Papa Bug, what did you do?"
"I dug in the dung, and I did it for you."
"Papa, O Papa Bug, what did you find?"
"Ice cream and cake—but I left those behind."
"Papa, O Papa Bug, what will we eat?"
"It's gummy, it's yummy, it's dung! What a treat."

BOINK! "WHERE'S IT AT? ARE WE THERE? WHAT IS THAT?"

BOINK! "IT'S A SKIN, BUT THERE'S NOBODY IN!"

BOINK! "WELL, THAT'S IT. I'M NOT KIDDING. I QUIT."

Rutabagas, red potatoes, cabbages, and beans,
Chubby, lumpy pumpkins and a clump of collard greens.
Grab and gulp and gobble-gobble—never get enough.
Cram it in there! Bust a button! Stuff, stuff, stuff.

Beetle has a bellyache, Weevil has a cramp.
Mama Pitter-Patter-Pede is belching like a champ.
Katydidn't, Cricket wouldn't, Hopper couldn't chirp.
All they do is roll around and burp, burp, burp.

Squeeze beneath a burly squash. Burrow underground.
Dig a little hideout where you never will be found.
Rain is coming. Cold is coming. Dig it really deep.
Then listen to the dripping as you sleep, sleep, sleep.

Drip—drip—wet and muddy.
Party's over, everybody.

Split—splat—plipping, plopping,
Ripe tomatoes dripping, dropping.

Plink—plunk—peppers fall.
Autumn rain will rot 'em all.

Ick—ugh—creeping mold.
Days are dark and nights are cold.

Wink—blink—close your eyes.
Dream of sunny summer skies.

Splashing and splattering over the trails,
Wobbling, bobbling, here come the snails!
Mr. Mistake is ahead by a shell.
Who will the winner be? No one can tell.
Rounding the radishes, what do they find?
A big snaky smile with a belly behind.
Mr. Mistake doesn't see it in time—

Crunch! He's a munchie! A luncheon of slime.
Slippingly, silently, somebody passes—

The winner! The winner! It's Mrs. Molasses!

SPLAT!
That's that.